GRAPHIC AMERICA

FREE AT LAST!

JOHN PERRITANO

Crabtree Publishing
crabtreebooks.com

Crabtree Publishing

crabtreebooks.com 800-387-7650

Hardcover 978-0-7787-4185-5
Paperback 978-0-7787-4212-8
Ebook (pdf) 978-0-7787-8954-3

Printed in the U.S.A.
082025/CP20250806

Library and Archives Canada Cataloguing in Publication

Perritano, John
Free at last! / John Perritano.

(Graphic America)
Includes index.
ISBN 978-0-7787-4185-5 (bound).--
ISBN 978-0-7787-4212-8 (pbk.)

1. Slaves--Emancipation--United States--Comic books, strips, etc.--Juvenile literature. 2. African Americans--History--1863-1877-- Comic books, strips, etc.--Juvenile literature. 3. African Americans-- Civil rights--History--19th century--Comic books, strips, etc.--Juvenile literature. 4. United States--Race relations--History--19th century--Comic books, strips, etc.--Juvenile literature. I. Title. II. Series.

E453.P47 2008 j973.7'14 C2008-906285-X

Published in Canada
Crabtree Publishing
616 Welland Avenue
St. Catharines, Ontario
L2M 5V6

Published in the United States
Crabtree Publishing
347 Fifth Avenue
Suite 1402-145
New York, NY 10016

Author: John Perritano
Coordinating editor: Chester Fisher
Editors: Scholastic Ventures Inc., Molly Aloian
Copy editor: Scholastic Ventures Inc.
Proofreaders: Adrianna Morganelli, Crystal Sikkens
Project editor: Robert Walker
Production manager: Candice Campbell
Prepress technician: Katherine Kantor
Logo design: Samantha Crabtree
Project manager: Santosh Vasudevan (Q2AMedia)
Art direction: Rahul Dhiman (Q2AMedia)
Design: Tarang Saggar (Q2AMedia)
Illustrations: Q2AMedia

Library of Congress Cataloging-in-Publication Data
Perritano, John.
Free at last! / John Perritano.
p. cm. -- (Graphic America)
Includes index.
ISBN-13: 978-0-7787-4212-8 (pbk. : alk. paper)
ISBN-10: 0-7787-4212-1 (pbk. : alk. paper)
ISBN-13: 978-0-7787-4185-5 (reinforced library binding : alk. paper)
ISBN-10: 0-7787-4185-0 (reinforced library binding : alk. paper)
1. Slaves--Emancipation--United States--Comic books, strips, etc.--Juvenile literature. 2. African Americans--History--1863-1877--Comic books, strips, etc.--Juvenile literature. 3. African Americans--Civil rights--History--19th century--Comic books, strips, etc.--Juvenile literature. 4. United States--Race relations--History--19th century--Comic books, strips, etc.--Juvenile literature. 5. Graphic novels. I. Title. II. Series.
E453.P475 2009
973.7'14--dc22 2008041852

CONTENTS

WAR FOR FREEDOM

WHEN THE UNITED STATES BEGAN IN 1776, THE DECLARATION OF INDEPENDENCE SHOUTED TO THE WORLD THAT ALL MEN WERE CREATED EQUAL. YET, AFRICAN SLAVES DID NOT SHARE IN THE PROMISE OF THE NEW COUNTRY. SLAVES WORKED IN HARSH CONDITIONS UNDER THE CLENCHED FISTS OF THEIR OWNERS.
WORK FASTER... FASTER, SLAVES. YOU BELONG TO MASTER THOMAS, NOW.

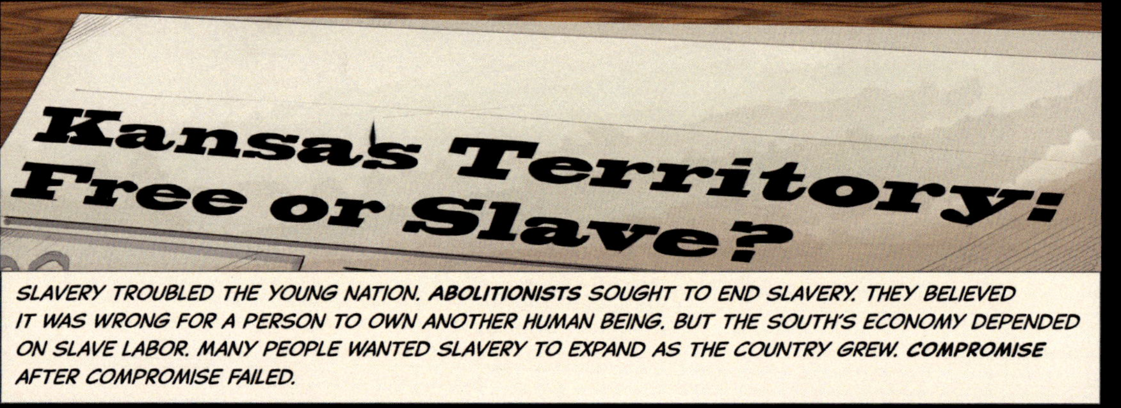
Kansas Territory: Free or Slave?
SLAVERY TROUBLED THE YOUNG NATION. **ABOLITIONISTS** SOUGHT TO END SLAVERY. THEY BELIEVED IT WAS WRONG FOR A PERSON TO OWN ANOTHER HUMAN BEING. BUT THE SOUTH'S ECONOMY DEPENDED ON SLAVE LABOR. MANY PEOPLE WANTED SLAVERY TO EXPAND AS THE COUNTRY GREW. **COMPROMISE** AFTER COMPROMISE FAILED.

NOW, IF IT BE DEEMED NECESSARY THAT I SHOULD FORFEIT MY LIFE ... AND MINGLE MY BLOOD ... WITH THE BLOOD OF MILLIONS IN THIS SLAVE COUNTRY ...SO LET IT BE DONE. *
WITH THE END OF SLAVERY NOWHERE IN SIGHT, ABOLITIONIST JOHN BROWN AND 21 OTHERS ATTACKED AN **ARSENAL** AT HARPER'S FERRY, VIRGINIA, ON OCTOBER 16, 1859. BROWN WANTED TO GET THE WEAPONS KEPT IN THE BUILDING AND GIVE THEM TO THE SLAVES. BROWN'S PLAN FAILED. AFTER HIS CAPTURE, A COURT FOUND BROWN GUILTY OF TREASON AND SENTENCED HIM TO DEATH BY HANGING.

*ACTUAL QUOTE

TWO YEARS AFTER JOHN BROWN'S RAID, AMERICANS CHOSE ABRAHAM LINCOLN, AN OPPONENT OF SLAVERY, TO BE PRESIDENT OF THE UNITED STATES. THERE WERE FOUR MILLION SLAVES IN AMERICA AT THE TIME, MOST OF THEM LIVING IN THE SOUTH. WITH LINCOLN AS PRESIDENT, THE SOUTH FEARED FOR ITS WAY OF LIFE.

THE SOUTH **SECEDED** FROM THE UNION AND FORMED ITS OWN COUNTRY: THE **CONFEDERATE** STATES OF AMERICA. ON APRIL 12, 1861, THE CONFEDATES FIRED ON FORT SUMTER, SOUTH CAROLINA. AMERICA WAS NOW ENGAGED IN A CIVIL WAR.

AS FIGHTING RAGED FROM MARYLAND TO MISSISSIPPI, PRESIDENT LINCOLN DECIDED TO **EMANCIPATE**, OR FREE, THE SLAVES IN THE REBELLIOUS STATES. ON SEPTEMBER 22, 1862, LINCOLN RELEASED THE EMANCIPATION PROCLAMATION.
I DO ORDER AND DECLARE THAT ALL PERSONS HELD AS SLAVES ...HENCEFORWARD SHALL BE FREE. *

BY THE END OF THE WAR IN 1865, THE SOUTH WAS IN SHAMBLES. AS THE CONFEDERATE ARMY RETREATED, UNION GENERAL WILLIAM T. SHERMAN SET ASIDE SEVERAL ISLANDS IN SOUTH CAROLINA FOR FREED SLAVES. SHERMAN GAVE EACH FAMILY 40 ACRES AND A MULE TO WORK THE LAND.
YOU ARE FREE NOW! GO LIVE LIFE AS YOU CHOOSE, BUT LIVE IT AS FREE AMERICANS.

*ACTUAL QUOTE FROM EMANCIPATION PROCLAMATION

ABOLISHING SLAVERY FOREVER

THE EMANCIPATION PROCLAMATION WAS A TEMPORARY MEASURE. IT ONLY FREED THE SLAVES IN THE CONFEDERACY UNDER UNION CONTROL. PRESIDENT LINCOLN AND HIS SUPPORTERS WANTED SOMETHING MORE LASTING. THAT'S WHEN CONGRESS DECIDED TO ABOLISH SLAVERY ACROSS THE COUNTRY. TO DO THAT, CONGRESS HAD TO AMEND, OR CHANGE, THE U.S. CONSTITUTION.
FELLOW SENATORS, GENTLEMEN, AND FRIENDS...SLAVERY MUST BE ABOLISHED NOW AND FOREVER. THE TIME HAS COME TO RID THIS NATION OF THIS TERRIBLE STAIN.

FOR DECADES, CONGRESS HAD MADE LAWS TO PROTECT SLAVERY, RATHER THAN END IT. FOUR YEARS OF WAR CHANGED ALL THAT. LINCOLN CHARMED INDIVIDUAL SENATORS AND URGED THEM TO OUTLAW SLAVERY BY VOTING FOR THE THIRTEENTH AMENDMENT TO THE U.S. CONSTITUTION.
DEAR SENATOR, WE, AS A NATION, HAVE THE OPPORTUNITY TO FREE A RACE OF PEOPLE FROM UNHOLY BONDAGE. IT IS YOUR JOB, NAY, YOUR DUTY, TO HELP IN THIS QUEST.
BUT MR. PRESIDENT...

ROCERIES
WE ARE IN FOR A HEAP OF CHANGE NOW.
YUP, A HEAP OF CHANGE.
SLAVE BILL
THE U.S. SENATE PASSED THE THIRTEENTH AMENDMENT ON APRIL 8, 1864. IT WAS NOW THE HOUSE OF REPRESENTATIVES' TURN TO VOTE.

WHEN THE HOUSE OF REPRESENTATIVES PASSED THE LAW ON JANUARY 31, 1865, THOSE IN THE GALLERY CHEERED WILDLY. EACH STATE THEN HAD TO **RATIFY** THE AMENDMENT, WHICH THEY DID. THREE YEARS LATER, THE NATION PASSED ANOTHER LAW MAKING THE FREED SLAVES U.S. CITIZENS.

WHAT NEXT?

PAPA, WHERE WE GOIN' TO?
I DON'T KNOW CHILD. BUT IT'S A BETTER PLACE THAN WHERE WE'VE BEEN.

BY THE END OF MAY, THE SOUTH HAD LAID DOWN ITS ARMS. THE CIVIL WAR WAS OVER. MILLIONS OF SLAVES WERE NOW FREE. PEOPLE DID NOT KNOW WHAT AWAITED THEM.

FROM SLAVE TO SHARECROPPER

WITH THE WAR OVER AND THE SOUTH'S **PLANTATIONS** RUINED, MOST FREEDMEN HAD TO WORK ON WHITE-OWNED FARMS JUST AS THEY HAD DONE AS SLAVES. THIS TIME, THE FARM'S OWNER PAID THE FREEDMAN A **MEAGER** AMOUNT OF MONEY, OR GAVE HIM A SMALL PART OF THE HARVEST. BLACKS WHO ONCE WORKED IN THE FIELDS AS SLAVES NOW WORKED AS **SHARECROPPERS**.
SILAS, TIMES ARE TOUGH FOR BOTH OF US, SON. THE WAR WAS HARD ON MY FAMILY AND ME. YOU WORK THE FARM LIKE YOU USED TO, AND I'LL GIVE YOU A THIRD OF WHAT WE GROW.
ONLY A THIRD? THAT'S NOT FAIR. I GUESS I HAVE NO CHOICE. I HAVE TO FEED MY FAMILY.

YOU ALWAYS WERE A HARD WORKING SLAVE, SILAS.
THE SHARECROPPER SYSTEM WAS UNFAIR. THE PLANTATION OWNER SOLD THE SHARECROPPER TOOLS AND SEEDS TO TILL THE LAND. HE THEN CHARGED THE SHARECROPPER RENT TO LIVE ON THE PROPERTY.

MOST SHARECROPPERS WERE POOR. THE FARM'S OWNER OFTEN LOANED THE SHARECROPPER MONEY AT HIGH **INTEREST RATES**. THE SHARECROPPER USED THAT MONEY TO BUY FOOD AND OTHER GOODS. IT WAS OFTEN HARD FOR THE SHARECROPPER TO REPAY THE MONEY.
SILAS, THE BABIES AIN'T GETTIN' ENOUGH TO EAT. I DON'T KNOW WHAT WE'RE GONNA TO DO.
HUSH NOW, LIZZIE. EVERYTHING IS GONNA TO BE ALL RIGHT. WE'RE FREE NOW. EVERYTHING IS GONNA BE FINE. YOU WAIT AND SEE.

GOVERNMENT ACTION

SINCE THE GOVERNMENT CONSIDERED SLAVES AS PROPERTY, NOT CITIZENS, THEY COULD NOT VOTE. THAT ALL CHANGED IN 1870, WHEN THE COUNTRY ADDED THE FIFTEENTH AMENDMENT TO THE U.S. CONSTITUTION. THE AMENDMENT SAID THAT STATES COULD NOT KEEP ANY MAN FROM VOTING BECAUSE OF THE COLOR OF HIS SKIN, OR BECAUSE HE WAS ONCE A SLAVE.

VOTING FOR THEIR OWN

FORMER SLAVES VOTED FOR HUNDREDS OF BLACK POLITICIANS IN THE SOUTH. MANY, SUCH AS JOHN ROY LYNCH, HELPED PASS LAWS PROTECTING PEOPLE'S **CIVIL RIGHTS**.
GEORGIA'S TUNIS CAMPBELL WORKED IN THE STATE **LEGISLATURE** TO MAKE SCHOOLS AND EDUCATION BETTER FOR BLACK CHILDREN.
HIRAM REVELS, OF MISSISSIPPI, BECAME THE FIRST AFRICAN AMERICAN SENATOR.

EDUCATION

BEFORE THE CIVIL WAR IT WAS ILLEGAL TO TEACH A SLAVE TO READ OR WRITE. AFTER THE CIVIL WAR, SCHOOLS FOR FREED SLAVES OPENED IN THE SOUTH. THE SCHOOLS WERE JAMMED WITH CHILDREN EAGER TO LEARN. TEACHERS FROM THE NORTH TRAVELED SOUTH TO TEACH THE CHILDREN.
WHO CAN TELL ME WHAT LETTER COMES AFTER "D"?

THE CHURCH

RELIGION ALSO PLAYED AN IMPORTANT ROLE IN THE LIVES OF FREED SLAVES. AFTER THE CIVIL WAR, MANY NORTHERN **MISSIONARIES** BUILT NEW CHURCHES IN THE SOUTH. BLACK CHURCH LEADERS SOON BECAME INVOLVED IN EDUCATION, GOVERNMENT, AND OTHER PROFESSIONS.
WE HAVE AN OPPORTUNITY TO BECOME ONE PEOPLE, ONE NATION UNDER GOD. LET US NOT DISAPPOINT HIM, BROTHERS AND SISTERS.
AMEN!

THE RISE OF THE KLAN

MANY SOUTHERNERS WERE ANGRY THAT THE CIVIL WAR FREED THE SLAVES. SIX FORMER CONFEDERATE SOLDIERS, LED BY GENERAL NATHAN BEDFORD FORREST, MET IN PULASKI, TENNESSEE, AND FORMED THE INVISIBLE EMPIRE OF THE SOUTH: THE KU KLUX KLAN.
THOSE THAT SEE US RIDE WILL COWER AT OUR FEET.
GENERAL, YOU LED US INTO COMBAT, AND YOU MUST LEAD US AGAIN.

MAMA, WHAT DID WE DO?
HUSH, CHILD...HOLD YOUR TONGUE.

AT NIGHT, THE KLANSMEN DRESSED IN ROBES AND SHEETS TO KEEP THEIR FACES HIDDEN AND TO FRIGHTEN PEOPLE. THE KLANSMEN BEAT, WHIPPED, AND KILLED FREEDMEN AND THE WHITE PEOPLE WHO HELPED THE FREEDMEN. THEY ALSO DESTROYED THE FREEDMEN'S HOMES AND FARMS.

CHASE 'EM BOYS, THEY CAN'T RUN FOREVER.
THE KLAN SPREAD INTO EVERY SOUTHERN STATE. SOME FORMER UNION ARMY SOLDIERS FOUGHT BACK. GOVERNOR WILLIAM HOLDEN OF NORTH CAROLINA ORDERED THE STATE MILITIA TO BATTLE THE "NIGHT RIDERS."

I'LL BE OUT IN AN HOUR, YANKEE. WE HAVE FRIENDS IN HIGH PLACES.
AS THE KLAN GREW IN POWER, CONGRESS PASSED A NEW LAW TO STOP THE GROUP FROM HARMING PEOPLE. IT WAS NOW A CRIME FOR THE KLAN TO RIDE AT NIGHT IN THE SOUTH. IT WAS ALSO A CRIME TO WEAR A MASK. HUNDREDS OF KLANSMEN WERE ARRESTED, BUT FEW OF THEM WENT TO JAIL.

BLACK CODES

VIOLENCE WAS ONE WAY OF ANTAGONIZING FREED SLAVES. LAWS AIMED AT LIMITING THEIR CIVIL RIGHTS WERE ANOTHER WAY. SOUTHERN LEADERS DID NOT SEE FREED SLAVES AS EQUALS. SOME STATES PASSED "BLACK CODES" THAT LIMITED A BLACK PERSON'S RIGHTS. FOR EXAMPLE, IN ST. LANDRY, LOUISIANA, AFRICAN AMERICANS NEEDED SPECIAL PERMISSION TO SELL THINGS.
I'M TAKIN' YOU TO JAIL IF YOU DON'T SKEDADDLE. YOU NEED A PERMIT, DULY SIGNED AND APPROVED, IF YOU WANT TO SELL SOMETHING IN THIS TOWN.

YOU JUST KEEP QUIET, 'CAUSE YOU'RE IN A HEAP OF TROUBLE.
WE WAS JUST TALKIN' ABOUT WHAT REVEREND PERKINS SAID AT CHURCH ON SUNDAY. SURELY, THAT'S NOT AGAINST THE LAW?
ONE BY ONE, SOUTHERN STATES CREATED THEIR OWN BLACK CODES, ALSO CALLED JIM CROW LAWS. JIM CROW WAS A FICTIONAL BLACK CHARACTER ON THE STAGE THAT MADE FUN OF AFRICAN AMERICANS. IN MISSISSIPPI, POLICE COULD ARREST BLACKS WHO GATHERED ON THE STREET TO TALK.

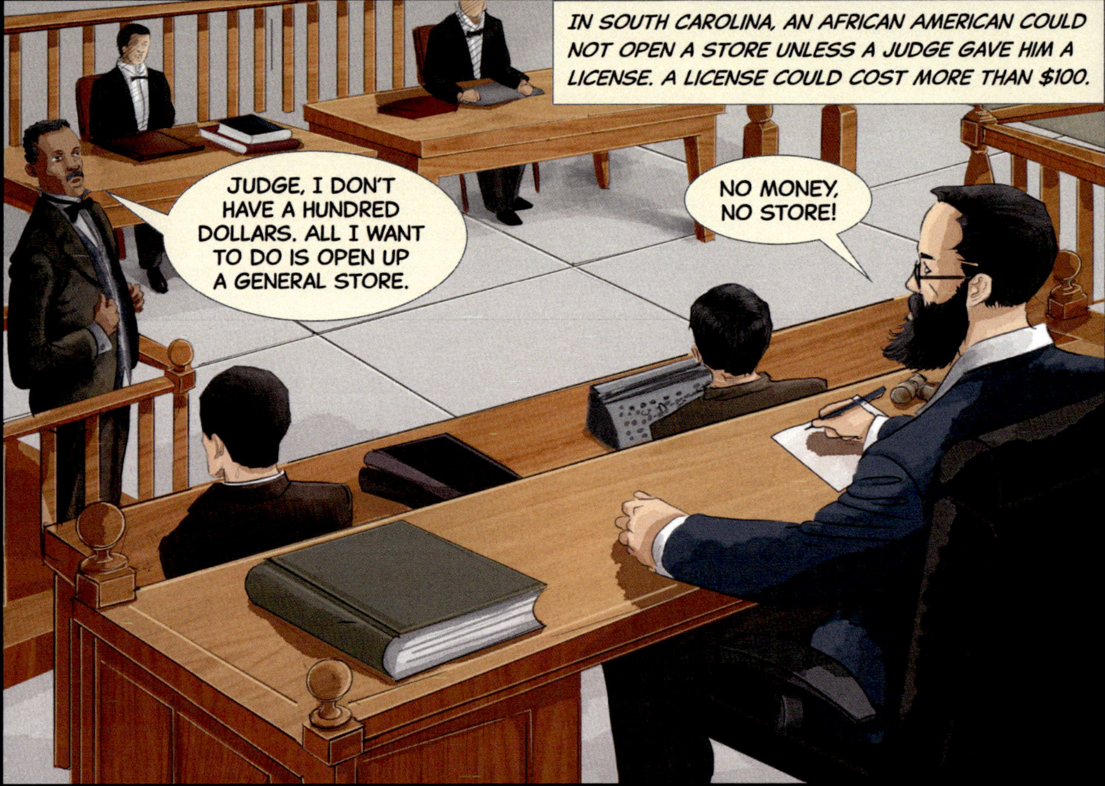
IN SOUTH CAROLINA, AN AFRICAN AMERICAN COULD NOT OPEN A STORE UNLESS A JUDGE GAVE HIM A LICENSE. A LICENSE COULD COST MORE THAN $100.
JUDGE, I DON'T HAVE A HUNDRED DOLLARS. ALL I WANT TO DO IS OPEN UP A GENERAL STORE.
NO MONEY, NO STORE!

IF AN **APPRENTICE** QUIT HIS JOB BEFORE HIS TERM OF SERVICE WAS UP, HE HAD TO PAY A YEAR'S WORTH OF WAGES TO HIS EMPLOYER.
I DON'T CARE IF YA'LL ARE MOVING TO JACKSON. YOU LEAVE NOW, YOU'RE GONNA PAY ME A LOT OF MONEY. DO YOU HEAR WHAT I'M SAYING?

IN SOME TOWNS, BLACKS COULD NOT RENT A ROOM OR OWN A HOME.
SORRY, I'M ALL OUT OF ROOMS.
ALL WE WANT IS A ROOM FOR THE NIGHT, SIR. MY WIFE IS TIRED.
ROOMS AVAILABLE FOR RENT

THE FIGHT FOR FREEDOM

CIRCA
WHITES ONLY
BLACK CODES WERE JUST MORE **DISCRIMINATION**. FOR 75 YEARS, SOUTHERN WHITES USED THESE LAWS TO BAR BLACKS FROM RESTAURANTS, HOTELS, TRAINS, AND OTHER PLACES. THE U.S. SUPREME COURT RULED IN 1896 THAT IT WAS OKAY TO **SEGREGATE** SCHOOLS AND OTHER PUBLIC PLACES AS LONG AS THERE WERE "SEPARATE BUT EQUAL" PLACES FOR BLACKS.

SEPARATE DID NOT REALLY MEAN EQUAL. DIFFERENT FROM WHITE SCHOOLS, MANY BLACK SCHOOLS DID NOT HAVE BOOKS, PAPER, OR EVEN A SAFE BUILDING. RAILROAD CARS USED BY BLACKS WERE NOT AS NICE AS THE ONES USED BY WHITES. THIS INEQUALITY ANGERED MANY CIVIL RIGHTS **ACTIVISTS**. ONE WAS FORMER SLAVE FREDERICK DOUGLASS. DOUGLASS AND OTHERS TRIED HARD TO HELP BLACKS ACHIEVE EQUALITY.
REBELLION HAS BEEN SUBDUED, SLAVERY ABOLISHED, AND PEACE PROCLAIMED...AND YET OUR WORK IS NOT DONE. *

BOOKER T. WASHINGTON, HIMSELF A FORMER SLAVE, ALSO HELPED. HE BELIEVED BLACKS WOULD TRULY BE FREE IF THEY RECEIVED AN EDUCATION.

*ACTUAL QUOTE

W.E.B. DUBOIS SPENT MOST OF HIS LIFE FIGHTING DISCRIMINATION AND **RACISM**. DUBOIS FOUNDED THE NATIONAL ASSOCIATION FOR THE ADVANCEMENT OF COLORED PEOPLE (NAACP), A GROUP THAT HELPS BLACKS FIGHT RACISM.

IDA WELLS COOK, THE DAUGHTER OF A SLAVE, WROTE ABOUT THE PLIGHT OF POOR BLACK CHILDREN IN SCHOOLS.

THE STRUGGLE FOR BLACK FREEDOM HAS MADE GREAT STRIDES SINCE LINCOLN FIRST FREED THE SLAVES. BUT PROGRESS HAS BEEN SLOW, TOO SLOW FOR MANY. WHILE THERE IS MUCH MORE WORK THAT NEEDS TO BE DONE, THERE IS ALSO HOPE.

TIMELINE

1863 – ABRAHAM LINCOLN ISSUES THE EMANCIPATION PROCLAMATION FREEING "ALL SLAVES IN AREAS STILL IN REBELLION."

1865 – THE U.S. CIVIL WAR ENDS, AND THE THIRTEENTH AMENDMENT, WHICH ABOLISHES SLAVERY, IS ADDED TO THE U.S. CONSTITUTION.

1865 – THE U.S. WAR DEPARTMENT FORMS THE FREEDMEN'S BUREAU.

1865 – RECONSTRUCTION BEGINS, REBUILDING SOUTHERN CITIES AND BUSINESSES DESTROYED DURING THE CIVIL WAR.

1866 – KU KLUX KLAN FORMS.

1868 – THE FOURTEENTH AMENDMENT, GIVING CITIZENSHIP TO FREED SLAVES, IS ADDED TO THE U.S. CONSTITUTION.

1870 – THE FIFTEENTH AMENDMENT, GIVING BLACK MEN THE RIGHT TO VOTE, IS ADDED TO THE U.S. CONSTITUTION.

1870 – HIRAM REVELS WAS ELECTED AS THE FIRST AFRICAN AMERICAN U.S. SENATOR.

1871 – CONGRESS PASSES THE KU KLUX KLAN ACT TO COMBAT THE ACTIONS OF THIS SECRET SOCIETY.

1877 – RECONSTRUCTION ENDS.

1896 – SUPREME COURT APPROVES "SEPARATE BUT EQUAL" SEGREGATION RULE.

GLOSSARY

ABOLISH TO BRING TO AN END

ABOLITIONIST A PERSON WHO SOUGHT TO END SLAVERY

ACTIVIST A PERSON WHO DEMONSTRATES OR USES CONFRONTATIONAL METHODS IN SUPPORT OR IN OPPOSITION OF A CAUSE

AMEND TO CHANGE

APPRENTICE A PERSON LEARNING A CRAFT OR TRADE UNDER A SKILLED PERSON

ARSENAL A PLACE FOR MAKING AND STORING FIREARMS

CIVIL RIGHTS THE RIGHTS AND FUNDAMENTAL FREEDOMS GIVEN TO A PERSON BY CITIZENSHIP

COMPROMISE TO SETTLE DIFFERENCES REACHED BY MUTUAL CONCESSION

CONFEDERATE RELATING TO THE 11 STATES THAT LEFT THE UNION IN 1860 AND 1861

DISCRIMINATION TO TREAT DIFFERENTLY ON A BASIS OTHER THAN INDIVIDUAL MERIT

ECONOMY THE SYSTEM OF FINANCIAL ACTIVITY IN A COMMUNITY

EMANCIPATE TO SET FREE

INTEREST RATE THE PERCENTAGE OF A SUM OF MONEY CHARGED FOR ITS USE

LEGISLATURE AN ORGANIZED BODY OF PERSONS THAT HAVE THE AUTHORITY TO MAKE LAWS

MEAGER NOT ENOUGH

MISSIONARY A PERSON SENT ON A RELIGIOUS MISSION SOMEWHERE AWAY FROM HOME

PLANTATION LARGE FARMS IN THE SOUTH

RACISM THE BELIEF THAT SOME RACES ARE SUPERIOR TO OTHERS; DISCRIMINATION BASED ON SUCH A BELIEF

RATIFY TO APPROVE AND ACCEPT FORMALLY

SECEDE TO BREAK AWAY FROM

SEGREGATE TO SEPERATE ON THE BASIS OF RELIGION OR RACE

SHARECROPPER A TENANT FARMER WHO GIVES A SHARE OF THE CROPS RAISED TO THE FARM'S LANDLORD

U.S. CONSTITUTION THE FUNDAMENTAL LAWS AND PRINCIPLES THAT OUTLINE THE NATURE, FUNCTIONS, AND LIMITS OF THE UNITED STATES GOVERNMENT

INDEX

WEBFINDER

HTTP://BIOGUIDE.CONGRESS.GOV/SCRIPTS/BIODISPLAY.PL?INDEX=L000533

HTTP://WWW.NPS.GOV/BOWA

HTTP://WWW.AMERICASLIBRARY.GOV/CGI-BIN/PAGE.CGI/AA/DUBOIS

HTTP://SCHOOL.DISCOVERYEDUCATION.COM/SCHOOLADVENTURES/SLAVERY/

HTTP://WWW.PBS.ORG/WNET/SLAVERY/

HTTP://WWW.PBS.ORG/WGBH/AIA/HOME.HTML

HTTP://WWW.DIGITALHISTORY.UH.EDU/MODULES/SLAVERY/INDEX.CFM